Arab

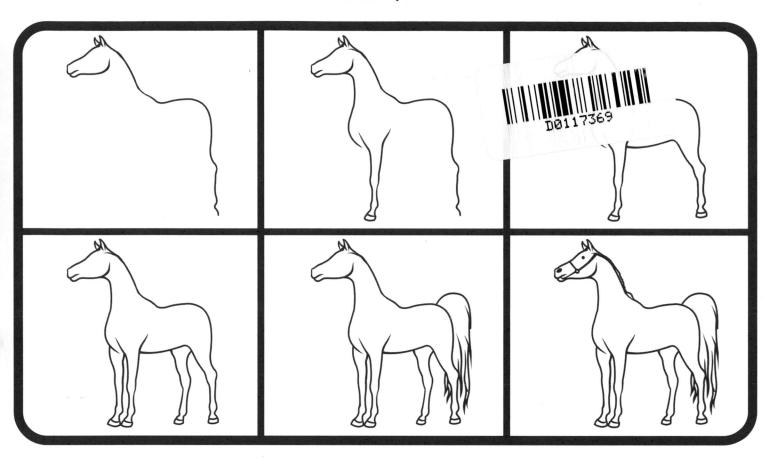

Thoroughbred

Friesian

Dartmoor

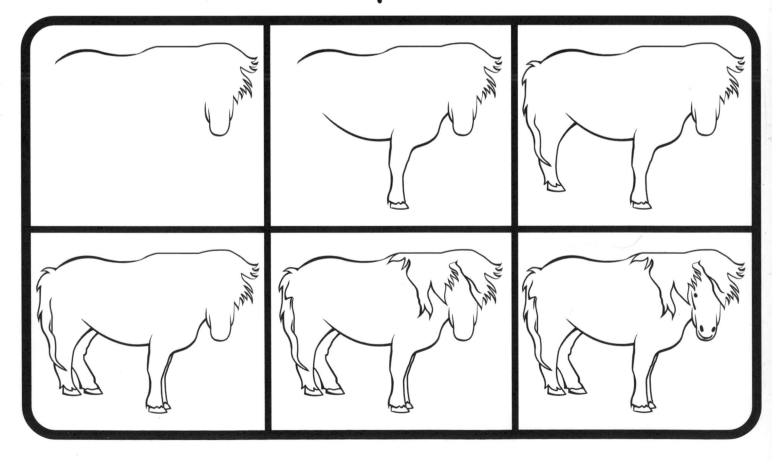

Lusitano

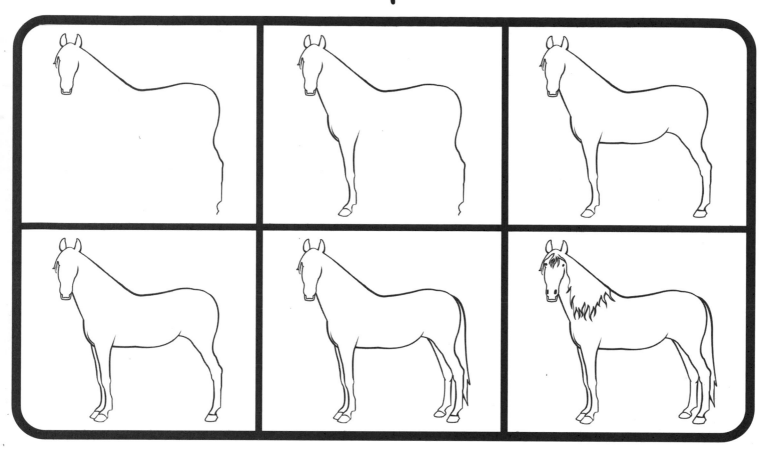

Lipizzaner

Mustang

Piebald

Shire

Falabella

Appaloosa

Shetland Pony

Palomino

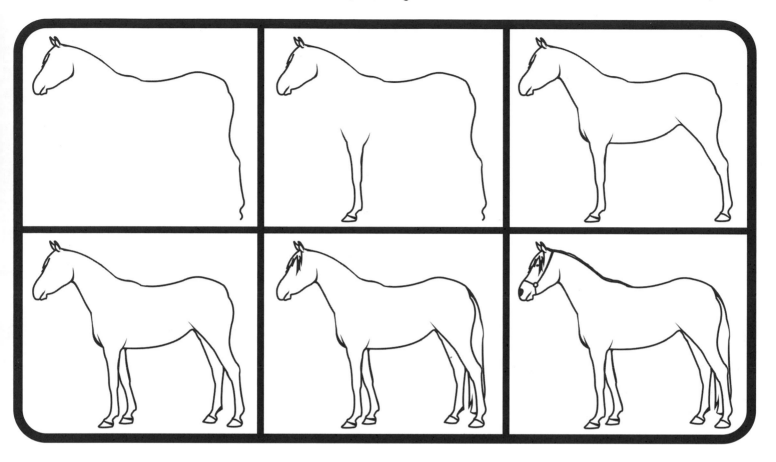

Norwegian fjord pony

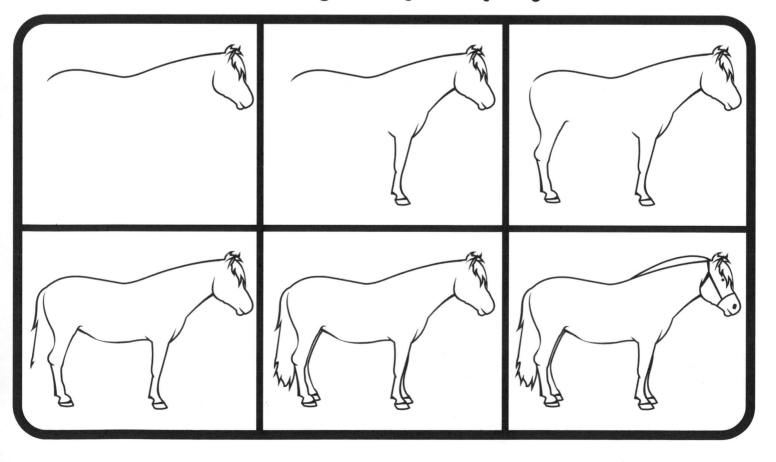

Breton

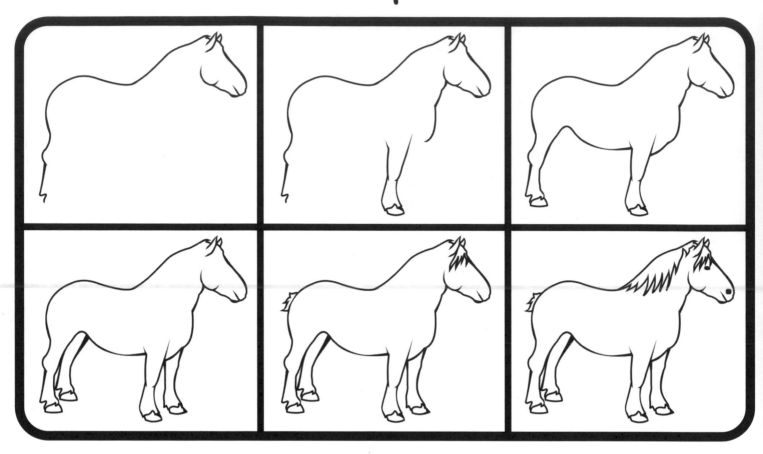

Pinto

Walking

Trotting

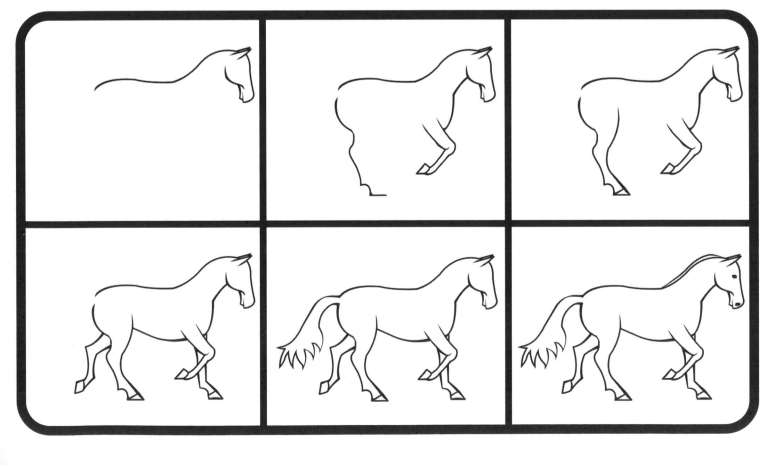

Cantering

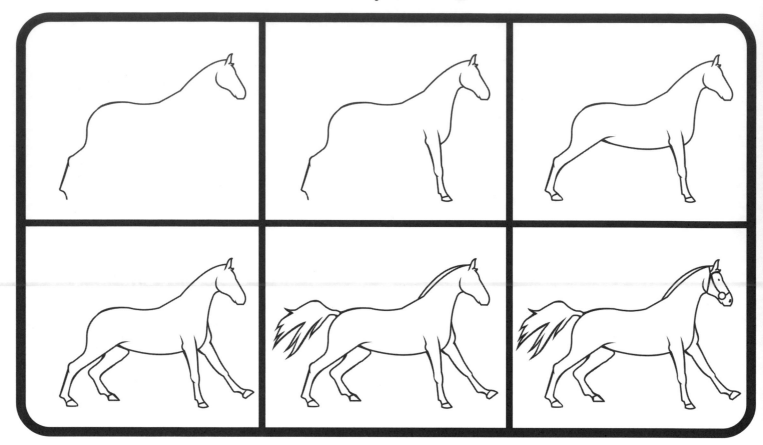

Galloping

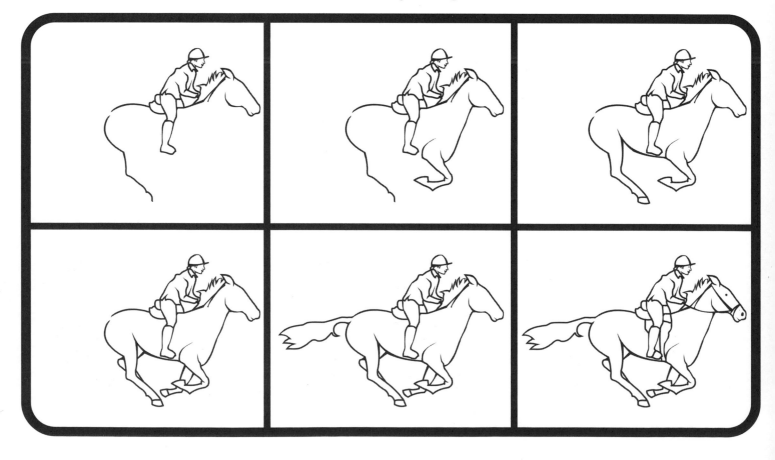

Jumping

Eating grass

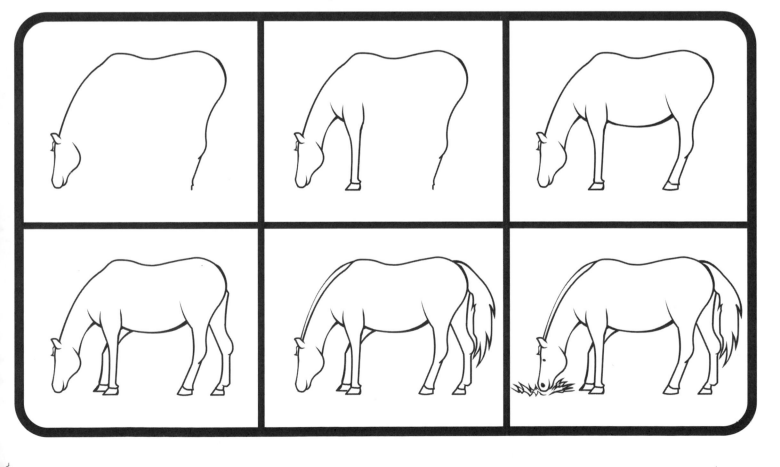

Rearing

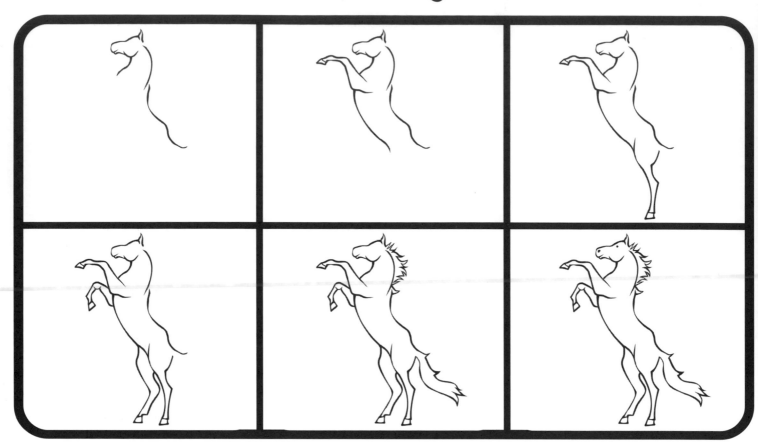

Tethered

Circus horse

Whinnying

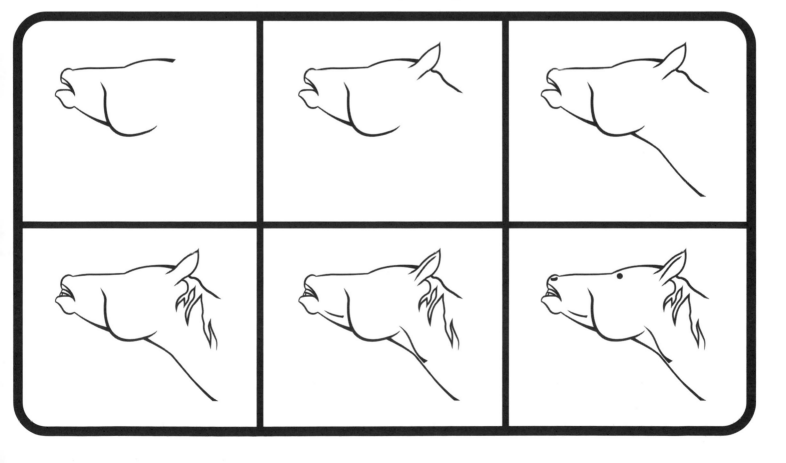

Prehistoric horse

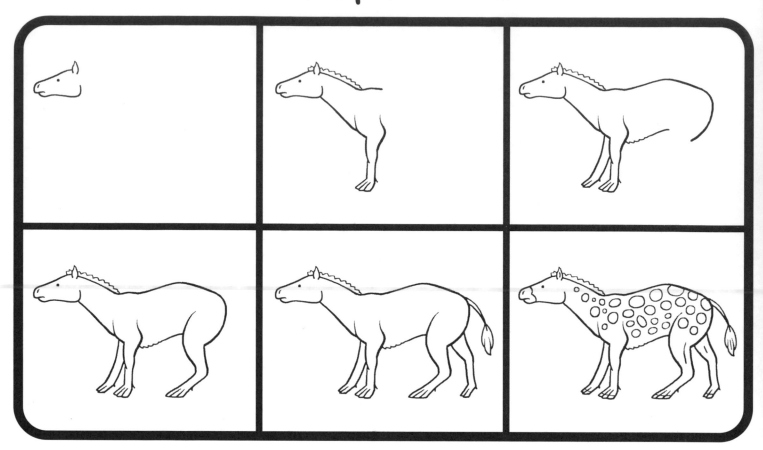

Horse and rosette

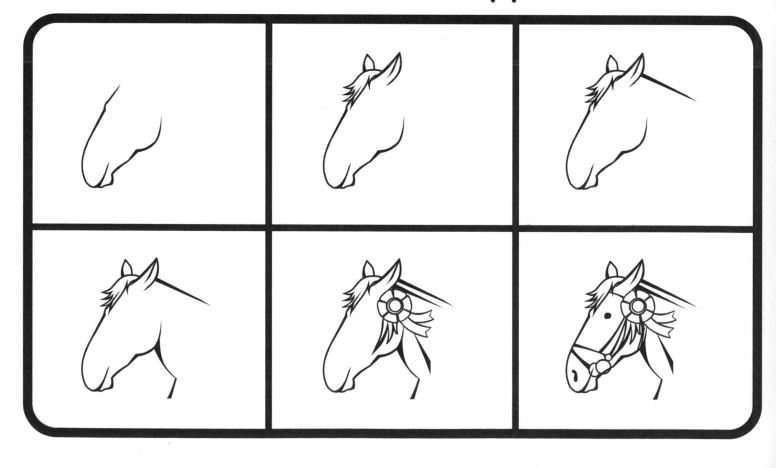

Dressage horse

Bridled horse

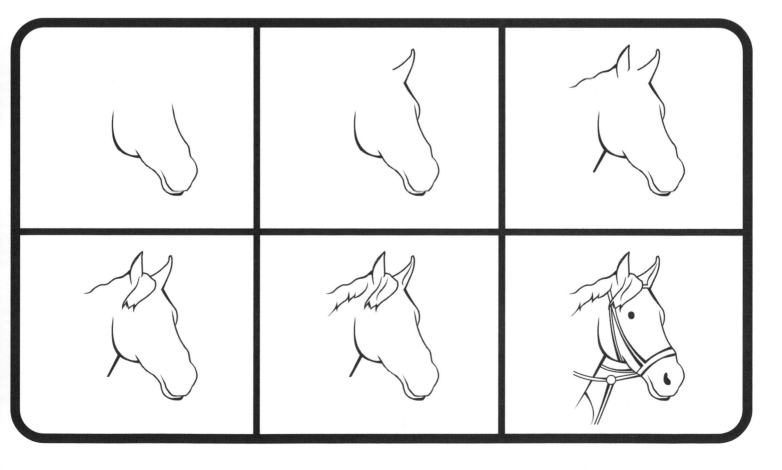

Bucking bronco with rider

Polo pony with rider

Mother and foal

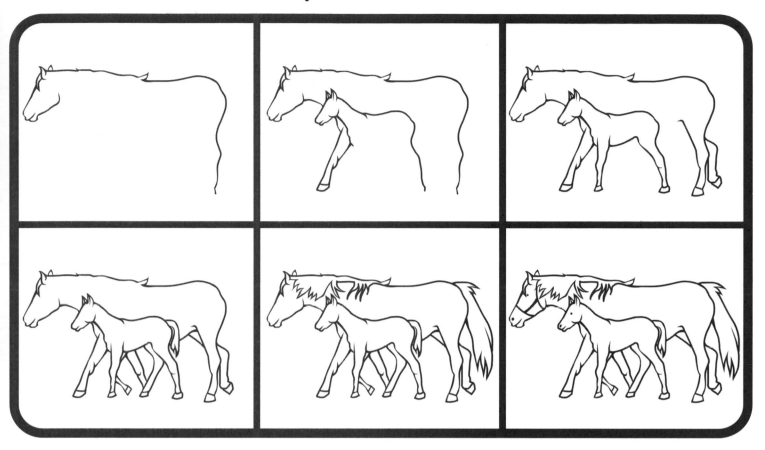

Racehorse with blinkers

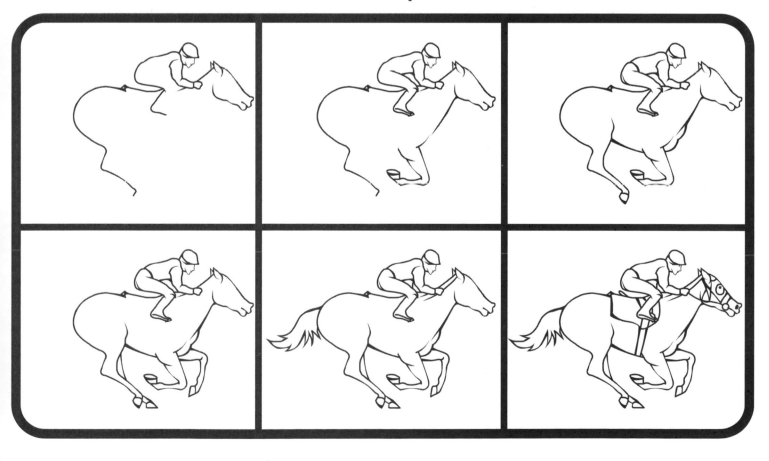

Medieval tournament horse

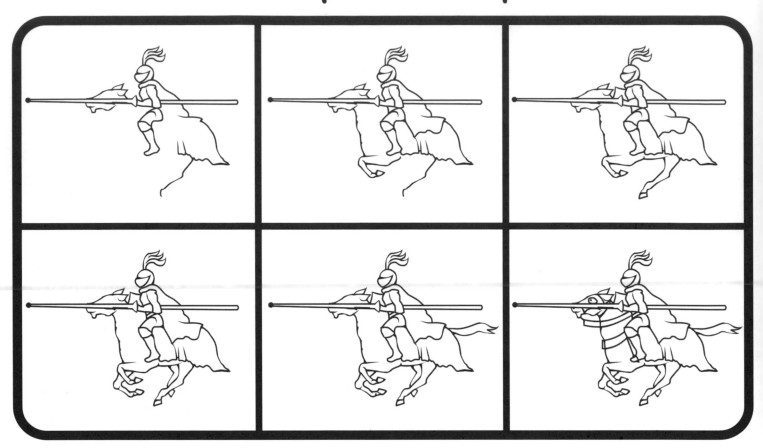

Expression; ears forward

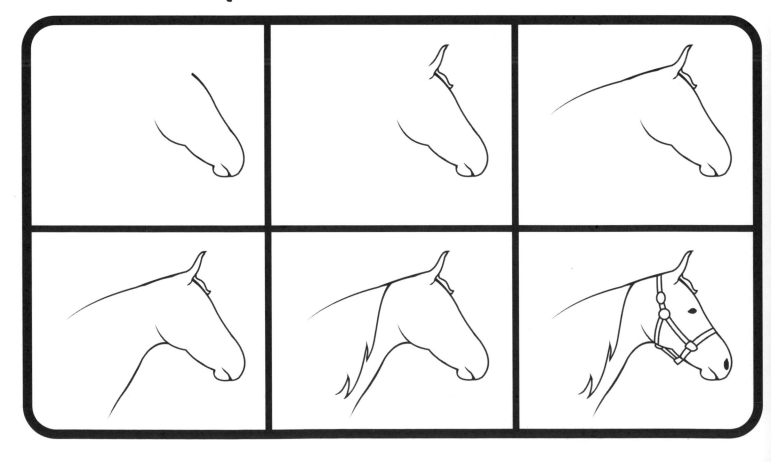

Expression; ears back

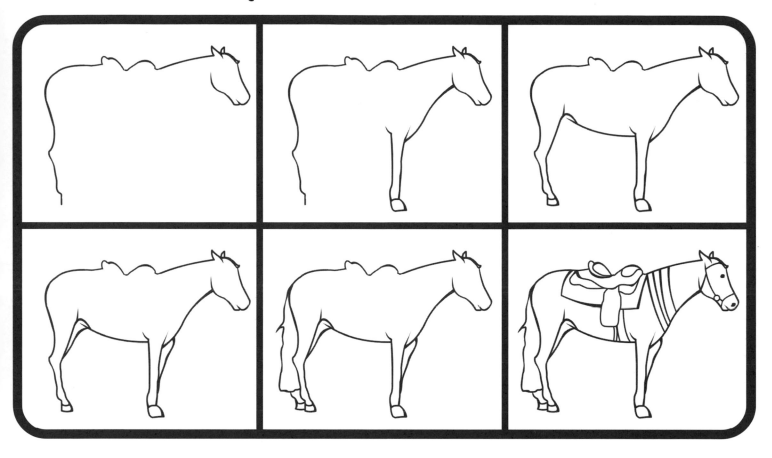

Harness racing

Classical equitation

Eventing horse

Two heads nuzzling

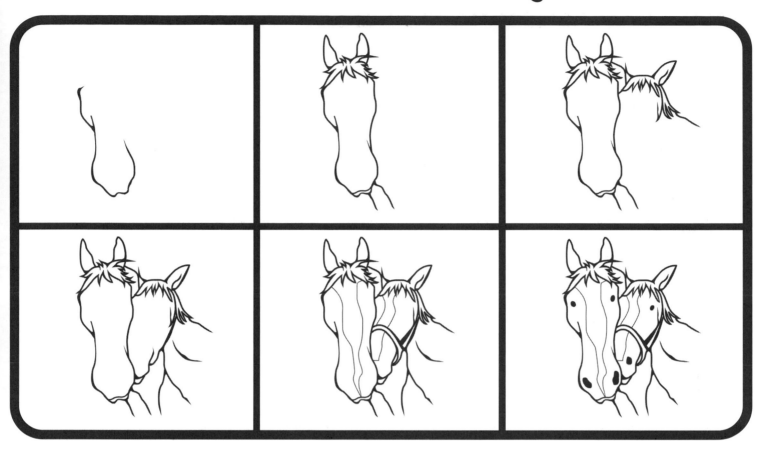

Show horse

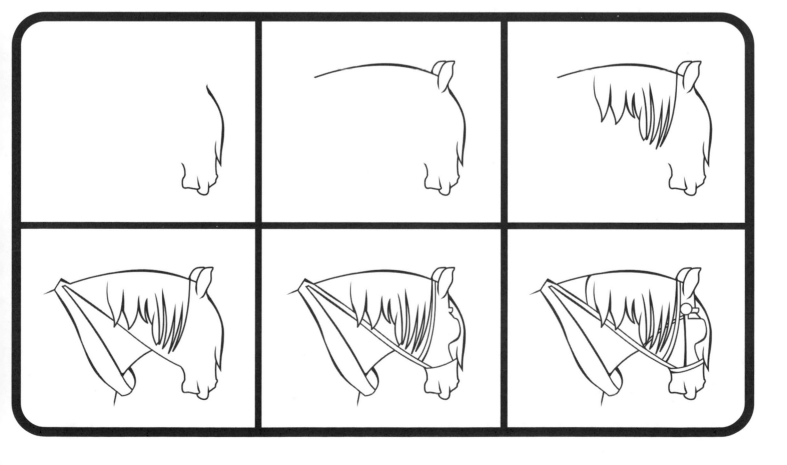

fantasy horse - unicorn head

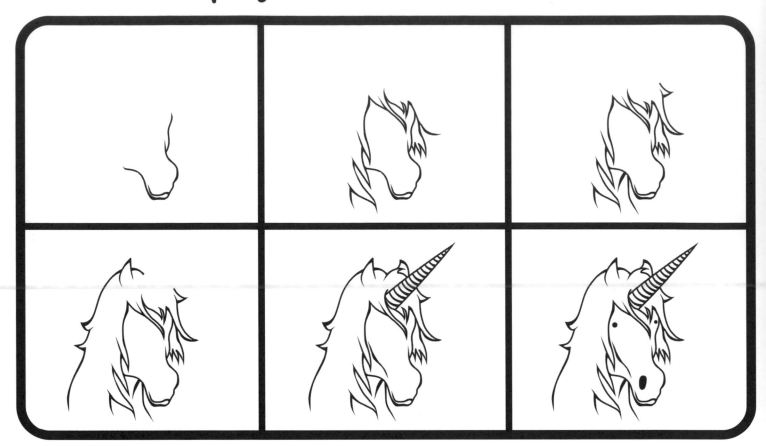

fantasy horse - pegasus full body

fantasy horse - pegasus head

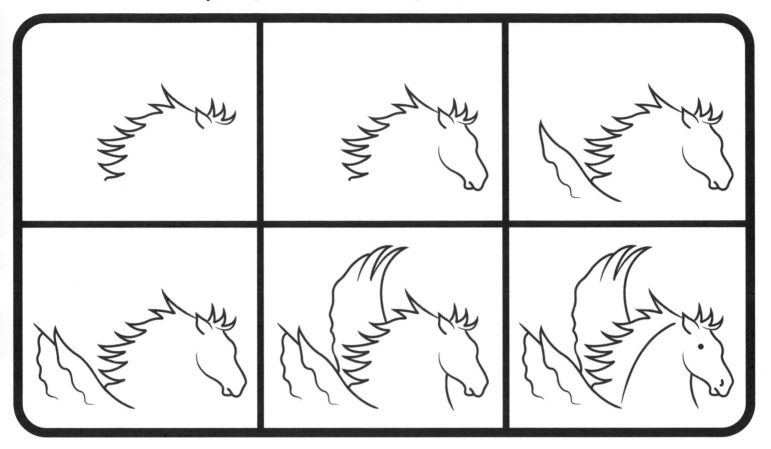

fantasy horse - unicorn full body

Mustang Close-up

Thoroughbred Close-up

Piebald pony

Eating hay

Plaited tail

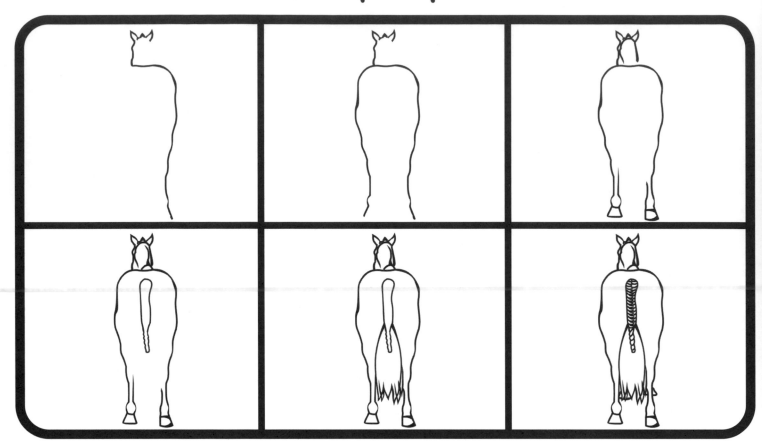

Plaited mane

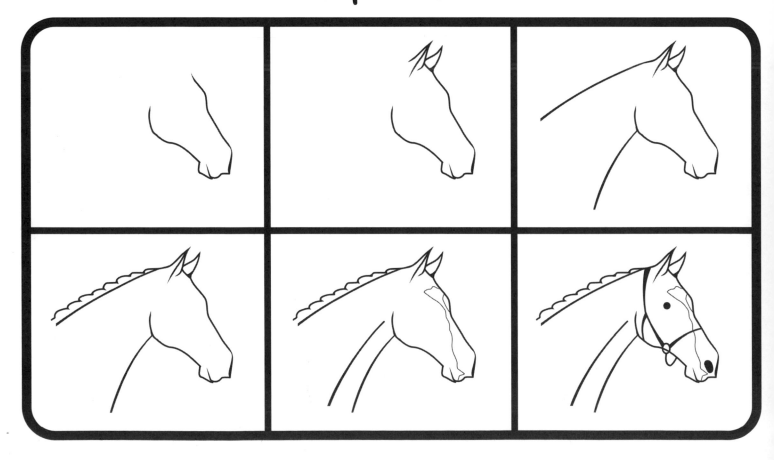

Horse in horsebox

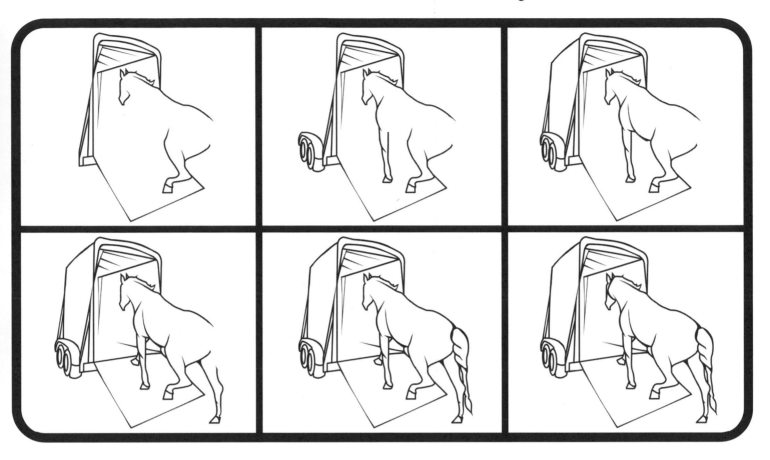

Rear view of saddle

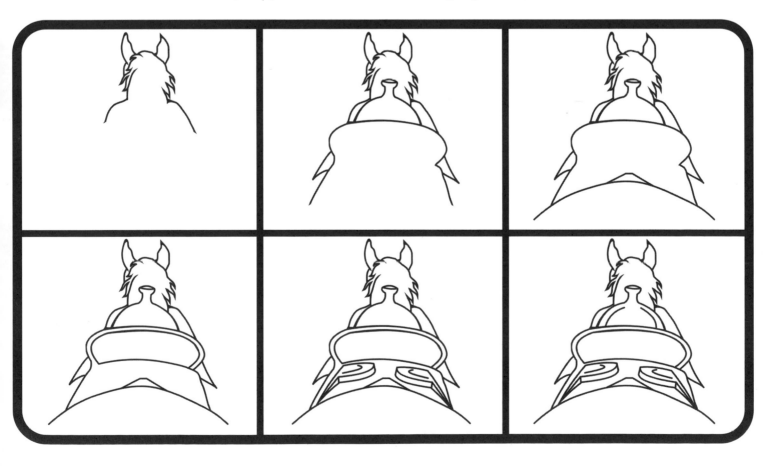

Horse lying down

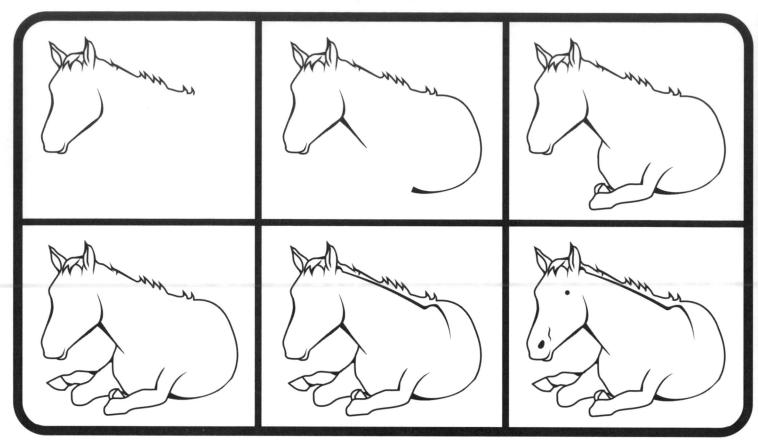

Horse rolling over

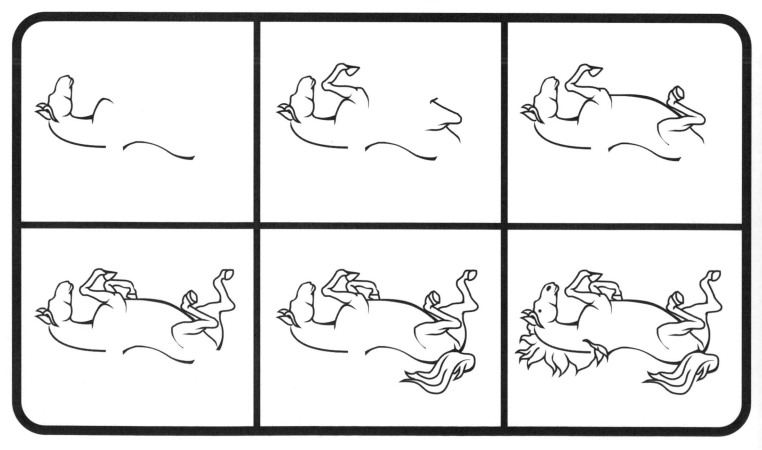

Horse pawing the ground

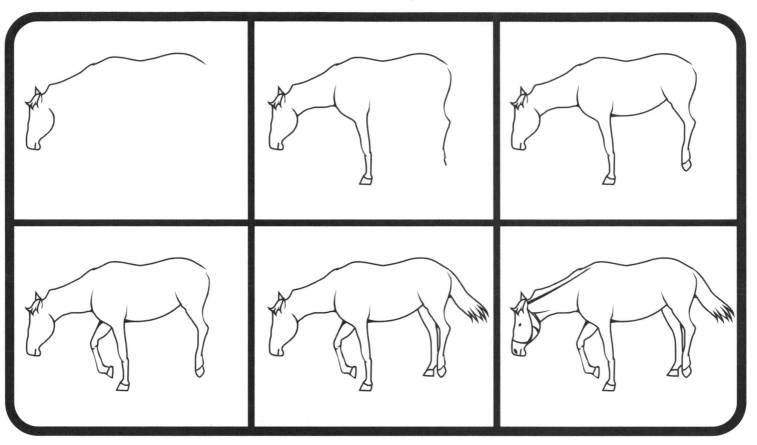

Horse with blanket

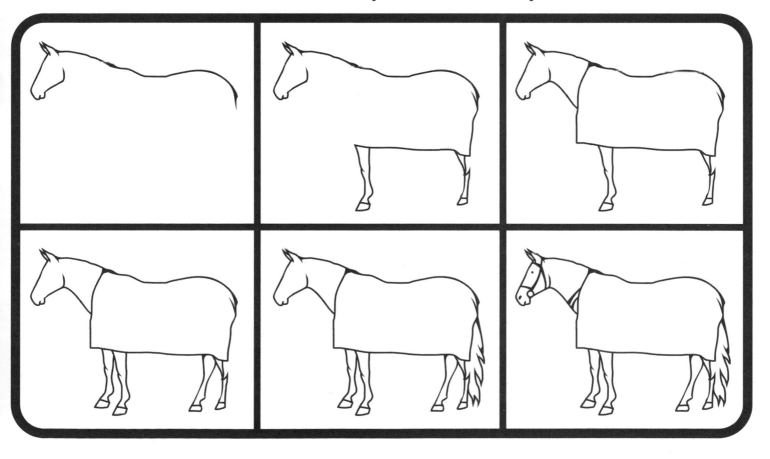

Foal

Horse being re-shod

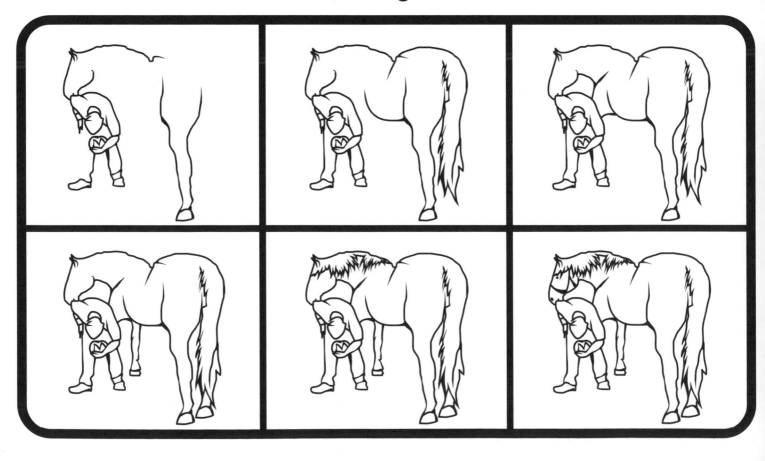

Horse led with halter

Police horse

Jockey on horse

Canadian Mountie horse

Horse drinking

Horse guards

Horse with Western saddle

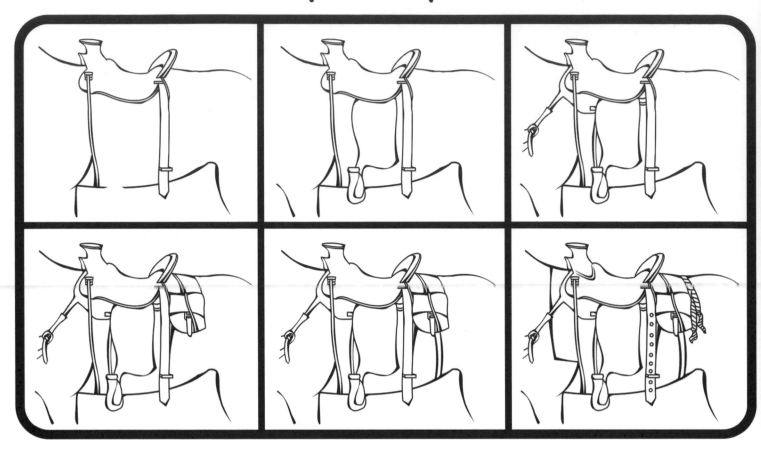

Horses with nose markings

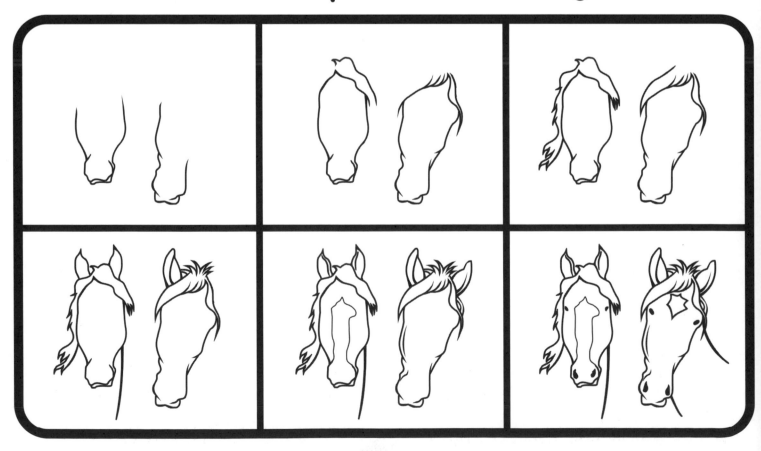

Show jumping

foal suckling mother

Play fighting

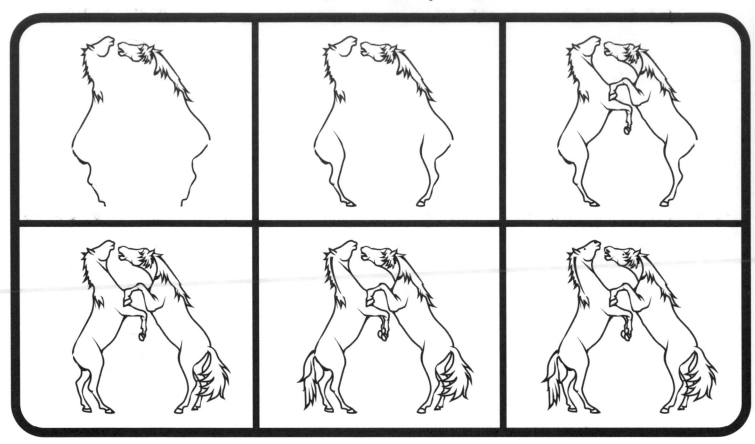

Horse jumping a countryside fence

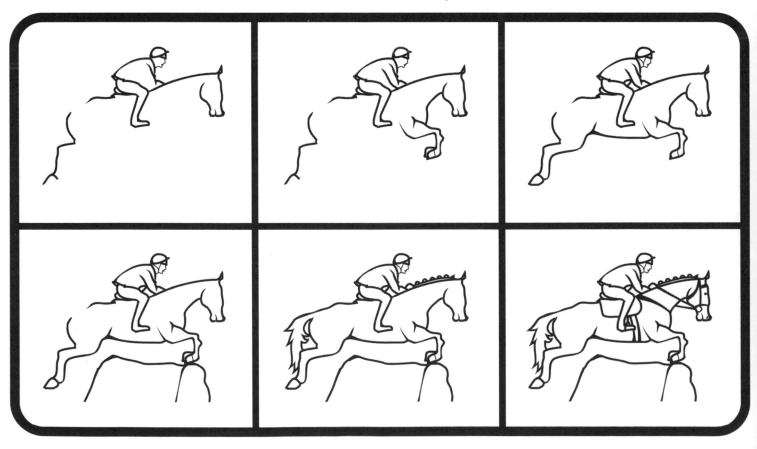

Horse trotting with rider

Buck-toothed cartoon horse

cartoon pony

cartoon seahorse

cartoon pegasus

cartoon horse - galloping

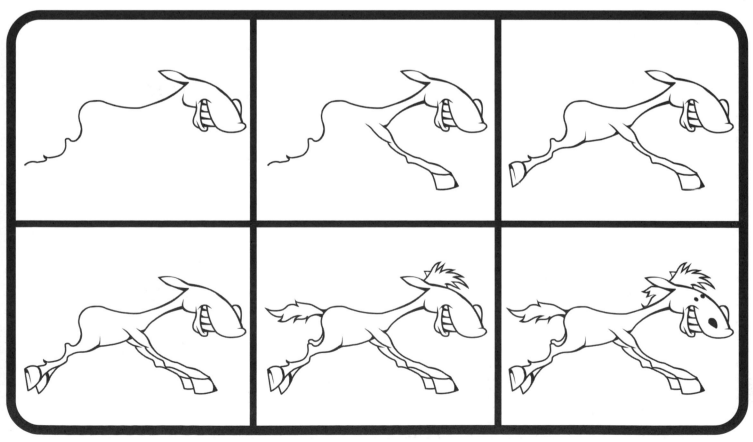

Cool horse

Cool pony

cartoon foal - cantering

cartoon old horse

Pop star pony

cartoon horse - flower in mouth

Horse over stable door

Horse – rear view

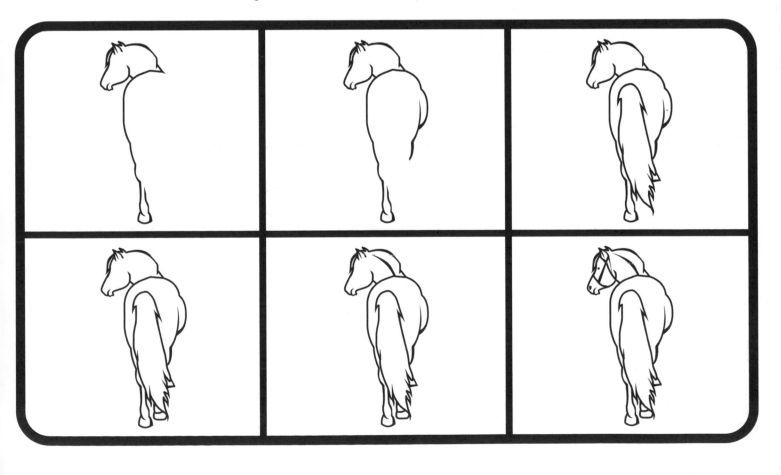

Jockey

Bucking horse

Horse Cantering through water

Horse high-trotting

Cowboy

Horse Chewing

Petting

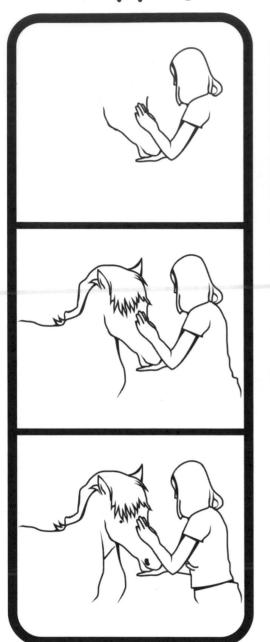

Horse and Cart

Horses fighting

Wild horse

Miniature

Horse with Native American

Peering

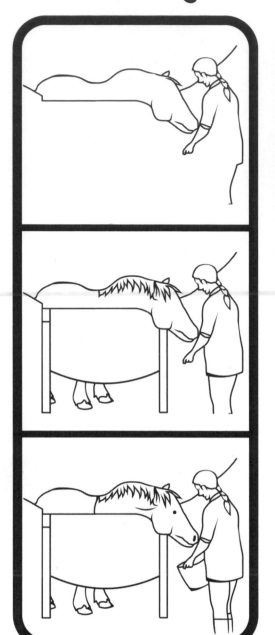

White-faced horse

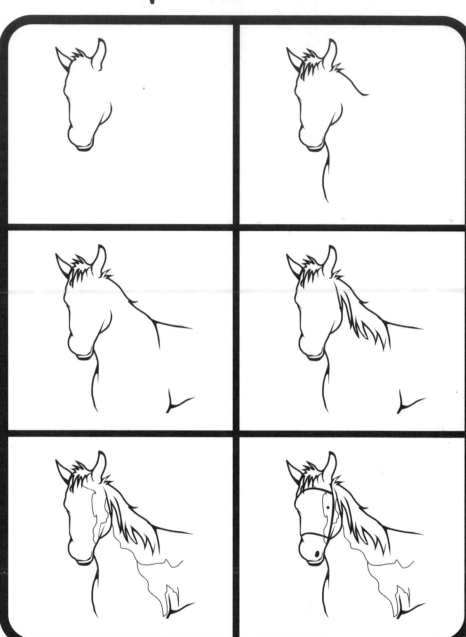

Leisure rider